Creating Home

Creating Home

Inspiring Comfort in Every Room

L i l y   Z a n e

Acquisitions Editor: Danielle Egan-Miller
Managing Editor: Jack Kiburz
Art/Design Manager: Lucy Jenkins
Interior and Cover Design: Scott Rattray, Rattray Design

Printed in the United States of America

98 99 00 10 9 8 7 6 5 4 3 2 1

Library of Congress Cataloging-in-Publication Data

Zane, Lily.
    Creating home: inspiring comfort in every room / Lily Zane.
        p.   cm.
    ISBN 0-7931-2966-4 (HB)
        1. Interior decoration—Psychological aspects.   2. Interior decoration accessories.
I. Title.
NK2113.Z36   1998
747′.01′9—dc21   98-29917
                                                                                    CIP

Real Estate Education Company books are available at special quantity discounts to use as premiums and sales promotions, or for use in corporate training programs. For more information, please call the Special Sales Manager at 800-621-9621, ext. 4514, or write to Dearborn Financial Publishing, Inc., 155 North Wacker Drive, Chicago, IL 60606-1719.

Contents

For Steve, who has given my heart a home,

and for Phil and Diane, for their powerful love.

Special thanks to Danielle, for her grace and guidance.

Dear Reader,

Whether it's a tiny studio apartment towering over an urban landscape, or your own spread on five acres, it's where you hang your hat. It's the place you call home.

While there are certainly innumerable practical things you do in each space in your abode, *Creating Home* aims to arm you with an attitude. It's the attitude to cultivate as you approach and explore what creates comfort, ease, and serenity for you in each room—in the space you call home. What makes you delighted, happy, serene at home? These tips and illustrations are designed to inspire you—to call up memories and images to help you envision your ideal living oasis.

You don't have to be the perfect handy homemaker, brandishing a glue gun and making every fern leaf perfect, in order to create a home space that reflects your ideas of comfort, joy, and delight. Let your own interests, personality, and treasured items shine through, and you and your guests alike will find a welcoming space that truly reflects its inhabitants.

I've tried to fill *Creating Home* with a wealth of inspirational ideas—for your entire home from the front door to the back porch, with special occasions thrown in. Using this book, you'll find ways to help you make every room special—more comfortable, more serene, and eminently more inviting for you and your loved ones, friends, and guests.

Wishing you all the comforts of home, a pleasant journey through these pages, and inspired trips through your own rooms!

Best regards,

Lily Zane

P.S. May your sense of well-being grow, as you create a home where *your* heart is.

Welcoming

"Where thou art, that is home."
—*Emily Dickinson*

HOME SHOULD BECKON you and your guests to step across the threshold into your own special place of serenity, security, and comfort. The feeling of home starts at the front door, so make sure your home's personality and style are welcoming, inside and out.

Make a glorious opening statement: paint your front door a different color.

WITH PAINT, a brush, and about an hour of your time, an ordinary door can become an extraordinary entranceway. A vibrant red door accented with a brass knocker and a shiny brass kick plate offers an elegant invitation to step inside. A fresh coat of a soft buttercream yellow paint can transform a simple wood door into a lovely portal leading to your own special sanctuary. If you can't bring yourself to paint your entire front door a new color, paint only the trim to give your entrance a quick face-lift. Just a small splash of a new color can create a fresh look that says, "welcome home."

Use colorful accents of flora, like a delicate wreath of bittersweet vine or a basket of seasonal greens, to continue your welcoming color theme.

IN SUMMER, a terra-cotta pot overflowing with vibrant pink geraniums, set next to the front door, offers a festive invitation to step inside. In winter months, that same terra-cotta pot filled with clips of evergreen branches and sprigs of fresh holly adds an eye-catching splash of color to the drab winter landscape. (Anchor your bundle of winter greens to a brick with twine before placing it in the pot, so it isn't carried away by a gust of wind.)

4

Express your personal style with hardware.

WITH JUST A few quick turns of a screwdriver, a plain old mailbox, doorknob, or knocker can be replaced with a decorative yet functional alternative. A whimsical cow mailbox? A hand-hammered iron key latch? Why not? New hardware is a small detail that's sure to make a big impression.

Use the numbers on your house to say something about your likes, your hobbies, and your eccentricities.

CLASSIC BRASS numbers, exquisite hand-painted tiles, even a plaque that includes a silhouette of your family pet—all make it easy for friends and family to find you, while serving as wonderful expressions of your personality.

Learn to mix functionality with personality.

THE FIRST STEPS inside of your home provide a sneak peek of what's to come, so find unique uses for ordinary things to make a strong first impression. Showcase umbrellas and walking sticks in an oversized watering can (weighted with a brick), a brass vase, or a decorative outdoor cement planter. A collection of interesting hats—new or old, women's or men's—hung on simple hooks can change a plain foyer wall into a stunning visual landscape. You might even surprise yourself when you grab a hat to put on as you're going out the door!

Showcase your style.

WELCOMING

Create a space to drop your gear once you step in the door.

AN OLD DROP-LEAF table, a sideboard, or even a small painted dresser with an endearing family history can create a place where you can instantly leave your day behind. A silver tray makes a distinctive catchall for the day's mail. Baskets and boxes have the advantage of making the clutter go away with the flip of a lid. Be sure to establish a special place for your keys—maybe a small antique trophy cup, a simple ceramic dish, or a pegboard stenciled with a favorite motif.

7

Design your own signature home aroma.

POTPOURRI, ROOM FRAGRANCE, or incense, used with a light hand, can infuse your entranceway with enticing, welcoming aromas that might linger for a few days. Experiment with lots of different scents and products to create an aroma that you will long associate with the feeling of walking in your front door. Or try your hand at aromatherapy, with scented candles or essential oils, to put you—and your guests—at ease the moment you step inside. Lavender, chamomile, and rose are calming scents. Mint and sage help to relieve stress. Essences of jasmine, rosemary, lemongrass, and balsam help to stimulate and refresh.

Stir potpourri as you pass by to release its scent.

Comfort:
The Living Room

"Home is a name, a word, it is a strong one; stronger than
magician ever spoke, or spirit ever answered to, in
the strongest conjuration."
—*Charles Dickens*

AN INVITING SPACE where you—and your guests—can
kick back, relax, and enjoy life is essential in every
home. Make sure your primary living space promotes
comfort, contented well-being, and tranquil ease.

Practice light artistry.

YOU CAN CHANGE the mood of your living space dramatically by changing the bulbs in your lamps or fixtures. Frosted, dim, three-way, full-spectrum bulbs, and halogens, all cast different tones of light. *How* you light makes a difference, too. When light shimmers upward (a small can light in a corner or a tall torchère), a room can feel suddenly taller and ready to wrap you in a warm embrace. Consider, too, using table lamps in rooms with ample overhead lighting to create intimate, inviting pools of light. Make sure your space is bathed in a soothing glow, so that you can leave the glare of your day behind.

CREATING HOME

Set your mood with music.

MAKE YOUR COMFORT space more inviting by adding soft strains of music to your daily routine. Relax with something soothing to cap off a stressful day. Or crank up music with a beat to stretch, dance, and leave your cares behind.

Use music to wash your living space with vibrant energy.

Commune with nature by bringing the great outdoors in.

A TRIO OF ROCKS collected on a hike, an interestingly shaped piece of bark or a grouping of vibrant autumn leaves can all be reminders of the beauty, tranquility, colors, shapes, and textures of the natural world. Display your outdoor discoveries on a bookshelf or table. Or better yet, plant them in a miniature meditation garden. Place a few of your organic finds in a simple saucer filled with sand to create a calming focus point that will help you leave the stress and tension of the day behind.

Celebrate your favorite season any time of the year.

THE STARK SIMPLICITY of a row of dried starfish on a mantle or window ledge can bring the calm of clear summer days to mind—even if August is already months past. Aromatic potted herbs or a Japanese urn overflowing with fresh cut flowers in rich burgundy, orange, and gold tones might remind you of the bountiful harvests of early fall. Set your own seasonal clock by surrounding yourself with a few comforting reminders of your most favorite time of year.

Make sure your floors are washed in color.

YOU DON'T NEED to have gleaming hardwood floors to enjoy the dramatic presentation of area rugs. Laid over wall-to-wall carpeting, area rugs inject not only color, but layers of softness. Add rugs wherever you want to draw the eye—underneath a favorite side table, in front of a fireplace, or directly in front of stair risers. Or, use a larger area rug as the focal point of a room, arranging your furniture around it to create an intimate conversation space. White rugs or sisal mats will give a cooler feel in the hot months. Remember, read labels on area rugs before placing them over carpet, as certain dyes may run. Then, get creative with color, pattern, textures, layers.

CREATING HOME

Keep family and friends close by.

PHOTOS ARE REMINDERS of special people, moments, and occasions, so don't overlook the magic they can bring to your living room. Whether displayed in abundance on a console table or scattered strategically around a room, keep your most cherished memories close at hand. Coordinate a collection of matching frames or mix eclectic sizes, shapes, and themes—as varied as the people and places in the pictures.

Display the great times and special people in your life.

Show off your collections!

THE SPECIAL TREASURES you find yourself accumulating say a lot about you. The rule is, if you have more than three of anything, you are well on your way to becoming a collecting connoisseur. Whether it's books, teacups, seashells, textiles, or baskets, surround yourself with your collections so you and all who enter your home are in touch with what's important in your life.

If you don't have a collection, start one.

HERE ARE A few ideas: walking sticks, fancy clocks, pitchers, or plates. Dolls, toys, or teddy bears are old standbys, as are tabletop boxes made of tin, hardwood, silver, ceramic, or porcelain. Book collections are a natural, especially when paired with unusual bookends.

Make candles a part of your everyday life.

CANDLES CAN TRANSFORM an ordinary living room into an intimate salon, warmed by a muted, soft light. Candles can sparkle and glitter on a silver tray or coaster or can be subtle and spartan in miniature clay pots. A collection of slim, white tapers in an array of glass, ceramic, and crystal candlesticks and grouped on a mantle or sideboard make an excellent alternative to a fireplace! A large multiwicked aromatherapy candle fits perfectly on a pretty but chipped china plate (salvaged from the back of the china cabinet or discovered at a thrift store) and fills your room with a subtle scent. Candles make your living room a space that feels good to be in. After all, isn't this what a "living" room should be?

*Appreciate the value and beauty in all
that is touched by hands that create.*

FIND A SPECIAL handmade item and give it a place of
prominence in your living area; acknowledging the creations of
others within your comfort space can inspire feelings of well
being and remind you of your heritage. A needlepoint or
handcrafted pillow can add personality to any piece of furniture,
especially if it's one you've made yourself. An ivory crocheted
throw or lovingly hand-knit red blanket might be tribute to
Mom's handiwork, and a welcome friend on a chilly evening.
A piece of heirloom, hand-tatted lace displayed on a tabletop is
a testament to the intricate handiwork of its maker.

Create new uses for ordinary things.

NOT EVERYTHING IN your comfort space has to be perfectly matched, part of a set, or evidence of a particular design school or style. Get adventurous and put everyday objects to use in intriguing and inspiring ways—after all, it's your space. Architectural details (old mantles, shelves, window sashes) salvaged from tag sales or second-hand shops make perfect display cases for your treasured collections. A rustic wooden cranberry crate can hold kindling next to the fireplace. A child's small wooden chair can double as a plant pedestal. Give yourself permission to use things you like for purposes other than those for which they were originally made.

Ingredients:
The Kitchen

"Cooking is like love. It should be entered into
with abandon or not at all."

—*Harriet Van Horn*

THE BUSTLING ENERGY, the enticing aromas, the subtle sounds of a simmering pot of soup being stirred on the stove or of busy hands kneading bread dough—these are what naturally draw people to the kitchen, the social center of the household, where work, play, family, friends, and pets all converge to participate in the pleasing and familiar rituals of preparing (and eating) a meal. The kitchen is your home's ultimate creative center, and it should welcome all who enter it.

Infuse your kitchen with treasured reminders of kitchens past.

MAYBE IT'S YOUR grandmother's heavy crockery bowl that always held the fixings for her homemade apple pie, now perched on your counter filled with ripening apples and pears. Perhaps it's a copy of your mother's favorite cookbook, anchoring your own collection of cooking tomes. Find a kitchen heirloom with special meaning and make a place for it in your own cooking space. Reminders of beloved kitchens past can serve as inspiration for new meals and nourishment yet to come. Let memories of the past feed your future.

Display a culinary heirloom to nourish your heart.

Have an extra seat handy.

PEOPLE NATURALLY GRAVITATE toward the kitchen, so make sure you have ample seating for those who drift in and linger while you're preparing tea for two or dinner for eight. A simple wooden stool, stashed out of sight in a closet or pantry, can serve as a handy resting spot for overflow guests. Paint the stool a favorite color that you'd never paint your kitchen—glossy brilliant red, shocking pink, vivid chartreuse—just for fun.

Because the party always ends up in the kitchen!

Marry music and food.

BRING MUSIC INTO your kitchen work space and then match your musical selections to what you're making or doing. A rousing aria from Puccini's *Tosca* or Verdi's *Aida* might fire your passion for making pasta. Smooth sounds of jazz can make tossing a salad or chopping crisp slices of cucumber and carrots a truly *cool* experience. Flamenco music might make for an inspired guacamole and salsa. Enjoy the precision of Bach when putting together a cake. How about kneading the bread dough to the melodies of Mozart? Smooth crooners like Frank Sinatra or Mel Torme are the perfect accompaniment for shaking martinis or stirring up drinks for a cocktail party. A small CD collection in the kitchen will add joy and flavor to any cooking experience, then match your mood and your task with your musical selection. Enjoy!

Let great chefs inspire you.

FRAME A MENU, wine label, or matchbook from a special evening of fine dining, and let the memories of that fabulous meal fuel your own culinary creativity. Or hand-write an uplifting quote about food, cooking, or living well, on a piece of heavy card stock and set it on a shelf near your cooking space.

Invite inspiration in its many quises.

Let form follow function and *be beautiful.*

EVERYDAY KITCHEN accessories—soap dispensers, crocks for utensils, canisters, paper towel holders, sponges, dish mats, dish racks, bread boxes—can be transformed into clever expressions of your personal style with just a little ingenuity and creative élan. Use a hand-painted ceramic soap dish or a terra-cotta wine coaster to hold your kitchen sponges. A beautiful aqua-green footed glass urn looks great on your counter, filled with wooden spoons. A favorite: find a brightly colored glass bottle, fill it with liquid dish soap, then cap it with a liquor-bottle pouring spout. Voilà! A decorative, functional alternative to that messy plastic bottle perched next to the sink.

Use your refrigerator as a canvas.

IF YOU'RE A clutter bug and like a crowded refrigerator front, upgrade to some new refrigerator magnets. Mini reproductions of old master paintings or classic sculptures, kitschy cows, fruits and veggies, or even Magnetic Poetry®—all can hold your important notes, reminders, and the kids' artwork in place while expressing your creative side. If sleek and uncluttered is more your style, mount a single postcard, a small illustration, or favorite photo with two-sided tape discreetly on the fridge, for a starkly subtle artistic statement.

Don't forget to change the images—maybe seasonally.

Fill your kitchen with rainbows on a sunny day.

HANG A COLLECTION of prisms that swing and sway and capture the light. Or, set a row of colored glass bottles on your windowsill to flood your kitchen with a spectrum of color on bright mornings.

CREATING HOME

Don't put away that screwdriver.

GIVE YOUR KITCHEN hardware—like drawers pulls, cabinet handles, doorknobs, hooks, and hinges—an updated look that complements your signature style. Even the pull chain on a ceiling fan can be accessorized with a decorative fob. Inexpensive and easy, new hardware offers an instant facelift in any room.

The smallest of expressions can make the biggest impact.

Change what can easily be changed—frequently.

UPDATE TIRED KITCHEN towels, potholders, rugs, and other linen accessories to brightly reflect the season, the holiday, or just your mood. Mix and match bright colors, textures, and patterns. Red and white checks, bright pink, purple and yellow stripes, polka dots, plaids, paisleys—the possibilities are seemingly endless and are easily affordable, to boot. If you're handy with a sewing machine, whip up a few of your own kitchen accessories with a variety of fun fabrics left over from other projects or raid the remnant bin at the fabric store.

A tisket, a tasket, every kitchen needs some baskets!

BIG OR SMALL, made of tied birch twigs or of stainless steel mesh, baskets are the ultimate decorative utility in any kitchen. Use baskets to gather ripening fruit on a countertop or to store root cellar items like potatoes, onions, shallots, and garlic in a pantry. Brimming with rolled colorful cloth napkins and silverware, a basket makes an attractive caddy on a kitchen table or breakfast bar. A favorite tip: The next time you're in need of a hostess gift, prepare a pie basket as your offering. Line a basket with a lovely floral dishtowel. Add your favorite pie recipe handwritten on a recipe card, the necessary fresh fruit or berries, and a decorative small jar filled with a favorite (or necessary) spice or flavoring—sticks of cinnamon, real vanilla extract, or delicate golden threads of saffron. What a thoughtful way to share the bounty of your kitchen with a friend.

Gatherings: Dining Spaces

"One cannot think well, love well, sleep well if one has not dined well."
—*Virginia Woolf*

THE BEST WAY to honor the tradition of gathering friends and loved ones together is by sharing good food. Celebrating a meal in a warm and inviting atmosphere can mend spirits, soothe the soul, and transport the participants far away from the demands of everyday life.

A divine room offers you the opportunity to enhance the act of fine dining, invite guests to linger at your table, and create your own traditions. Don't have a dining room? Make your eating space special, even it's just a table in the corner of your kitchen or a stool pulled up to a counter.

Honor the tradition of dining—anywhere.

ENJOY A MEAL in an area other than your usual dining spot—
perhaps in a space that's not even meant for dining. Dine *al
fresco* on a warm summer evening. If you don't have a dedicated
outdoor space or outdoor furniture, opt for something completely
decadent: Bring some inside furniture out and host an elegant
picnic in the backyard under the stars, complete with a table,
chairs, candles, and linens. For a romantic dinner à deux, set up
a card table in your bedroom adorned with a white tablecloth, a
vase of fresh flowers, and all the necessary trimmings; then enjoy.
Ordinary meals can become memorable adventures when served
in fresh surroundings.

Break out the finery—on a Tuesday!

HEIRLOOM AND OTHER special pieces related to dining—china, crystal, silver flatware, decorative platters and serving dishes, and linens—can add panache to the most ordinary of meals, even meals on the go. Try serving Chinese takeout or pizza on Grandmother's Wedgwood plates. Or use the decorative platter last seen on your table at Thanksgiving to present a hearty lunch of sandwiches and fresh fruit to your hungry crew. Simple fare is bound to be met with an enthusiastic reception if it's presented with thoughtful style and flair.

If your finest pieces aren't readily at hand, consider keeping a few special "duets" within easy reach.

FOR THOSE WITHOUT a china cabinet or sideboard in which to store finery, stashing just a sprinkling of special pieces in a kitchen cabinet or pantry is an excellent way to ensure that you regularly enjoy at least some of the beautiful items you own. Two place settings of sterling silver flatware can transform a spontaneous Sunday morning breakfast in bed into a truly elegant affair. Celebratory champagne sips much sweeter in lovely leaded crystal flutes at an impromptu cocktail hour. Fine English china cups, saucers, and cookie or biscuit plates are perfect details for an intimate afternoon tea with a friend.

Strive for casual elegance.

CANDLES, FRESH FLOWERS, and a centerpiece make any table look dressed up, even if it's just a small table for one. Use unscented candles so diners can enjoy the full range of flavors of the meal. An elegant white pillar set upon a plain white saucer will do. Use small vases, jars, or glasses for fresh flowers. Bright pink, yellow, and orange Gerber daisies look great in a ceramic vase. Yellow roses, clipped short and grouped in a

small, beaded silver-plated cup, are reminiscent of the English
country style. Whatever vessel you choose for your flowers,
make sure it's low, so diners can enjoy each other's company
through unobstructed views. Add a centerpiece as your finishing
touch. A footed bowl makes for the easiest, most versatile
centerpiece, as it can be filled with just about anything and will
always look good. Use fresh fruit, like a grouping of green limes
or of pale golden pears, pinecones mixed with pomegranates
and holly berries, or fill your bowl partially with water and float
fresh flowers or small candles in it—the possibilities are endless.

See your table through a child's eyes.

WHET A SMALL diner's appetite by setting a special place just for him or her. Colorful place mats and kid-friendly utensils make children (and their parents) feel like honored guests. Search tag sales for kiddie place settings, or use your imagination. Butter knives and shrimp forks are perfect for small hands, and dessert plates match the service of the grown-ups but prove a more manageable size for little eaters. Special place cards add the finishing touch. Remember what *you* yearned for during those seemingly endless adult dinners and be creative! A paper place mat and a box of crayons can keep little hands busy when adult conversations seem interminable.

Use cloth napkins every night.

NOT ONLY IS cloth an environmentally friendly alternative to paper napkins, cloth napkins make any meal feel like an event. You can make stacks of your own cloth napkins out of generous 20" × 20" hemmed squares of your favorite fabric. Extravagant ivory damask makes perfect accent napkins for an elegant, formal table. Bright tea towels that favor a particular season, holiday, or mood can be used, too, and they are mighty convenient for wiping up any errant spills. Napkin rings are a nice touch, as well.

Dress your table with signature style by crafting one-of-a-kind place settings.

MIX AND MATCH favorite pieces—plates of different sizes, patterns, and colors; odd pieces of stemware and glassware in an array of varying shapes, textures, and colors—to set an eclectic table that bursts with personality and energy. Or design a subtly detailed monochromatic composition by pairing heirloom salad plates with tag-sale chargers, or mixing thrift-store cups and saucers with a few of your very best dessert dishes, all in varying shades, textures, and patterns of the same color. Compliment these with matching linens, flowers, and candles as the final touches. Multipatterned or monochrome, both are easy, innovative ways to introduce your dinner guests to your signature or eclectic style.

Luxuries: The Bath

"Everything there is simply order and beauty, luxury, peace, and sensual indulgence."

—*Charles Baudelaire*

THOUGH A ROOM of utility, the bath is also an
intimate retreat where luxury and personal pampering
reign supreme. Your bath is a highly personal space,
so make sure that it reflects the things you like to see
and do. Treat the bath as an extension of your
lifestyle by allowing the colors, collections, and pieces
of art that inspire your senses of tranquility and
luxurious relaxation to cross the threshold into this
often overlooked room.

Go green.

HOUSEPLANTS ADD A touch of natural serenity to any bath. They also provide a lovely splash of color that conveniently fills an often-stark space. If you're lucky enough to have a window in your bath, welcome in an overflowing basket of glorious green ferns, which will thrive in the humid environment. If flowers are more your style, give your room a finished look with a small vase of fresh cuttings on a window ledge or countertop. Roses are particularly appropriate for the bath—once their petals fall, they can be collected and sprinkled into a warm tub for an indulgent afternoon soak.

An inspiring idea: evoke the calming sensation of the tide rolling in or waves gently breaking on the shore by incorporating sea treasures into your bath.

A SHINY ABALONE shell can serve as an unusual soap dish. A transparent canister filled with sea glass and shells perched near the tub might remind you of the glorious days spent at the shore many summers ago. How about a relaxing soak in a warm bath filled with natural sea salts? Organic reminders of water are particularly calming and comforting in the bath.

*Establish a place for everything and
put everything in its place.*

A PRACTICAL APPROACH to displaying or storing your collection
of *ecoutrements* is essential for maintaining the tranquility of your
personal oasis. A rainbow of bath beads is especially inviting
when displayed in a sophisticated decanter with a glass stopper.

A shiny aluminum sand pail might
remind you of summer days in the
sandbox, but it also makes a chic
catchall for your collection of
fragrant oils, bubbles, potions, and
lotions. Whether your style is sleek
and modern or casually eclectic, find
stylish vessels, baskets, and boxes to
keep your decadent personal products
neatly at hand.

47

Light a candle and treat yourself to a mood adjustment.

THE INTIMACY OF the bath is where you are most likely to benefit from the healing, restorative powers of scent. Aromatherapy candles not only smell heavenly, they also make beautiful decorative accents (tapers, pillars, wide triple wicks, and votives in a spectrum of colors) and emit a dreamy, indulgent glow when lit. Aromatherapy candles are the ideal complement to the room dedicated to personal luxury, calmness, and relaxation. Keep a variety of these candles handy in styles, shapes, and colors that fit into your design scheme. Here are some healing properties to keep in mind, as you make your candle selection: The exotic, heady aroma of ylang-ylang soothes and uplifts. Eucalyptus emits a stimulating camphor scent that is particularly beneficial when you're feeling dogged by a cold or just feeling drained. The light, flowery fragrance of lavender promotes relaxation and balance between mind and body.

Give your favorite accents a new home.

NOTHING ADDS PERSONALITY to a bath more than personal treasures, trinkets, posters, pictures, and art of all sorts. Keep the confines and the climate in mind as you find small *objets d'art* and wall hangings to complement your at-home retreat. A trio of miniature botanical prints looks lovely on a wall next to the sink. A collection of hand-painted tiles makes a colorful grouping on a windowsill.

 C R E A T I N G   H O M E

Express your personal style with hardware and accessories.

THE BATH IS a room filled with an assortment of hardware—from towel bars and shelves to paper holders and curtain rods—that subtly influences the mood of your special haven. Think of drawer pulls, switch plates, and other hardware items as you would buttons on a favorite coat—with only minimal effort and expense, you can remove the old and fasten the new to make a quick change and create an entirely fresh new look. Revising essential bath accessories, like waste cans, soap dishes, tissue boxes, rugs, and shower curtains, completes your bath makeover.

Sanctuary: The Bedroom

"Night with her train of stars. And her great gift of sleep."
—*W. E. Henley*

YOUR BEDROOM IS your personal retreat from the world. This space should inspire an attitude of total relaxation, comfort, serenity, and ease. Take the time to create your perfect retreat and make it thoroughly inviting on *your* terms. Whether it's a fluffy bed piled high with pillows or a spartan futon, cluttered or clear, your retreat should offer a welcome greeting and invitation for rejuvenation at the end of a day.

Make your bed appealing.

YOU SPEND CLOSE to one-third of every day in your bed, so make sure that it's an irresistible rest stop. Think about texture. How does your bed feel? Try purchasing the highest thread-count sheets in your price range and then bask in their luxurious softness. Or add a soft hand-crocheted blanket from Grandma or a lovingly worn favorite patchwork quilt for stylish extra warmth. Give your pillows a quick checkup. Are you happy with them? Do you have enough? A variety of shapes and sizes—like a neck roll, a small back pillow, a few square throw pillows—make great decorative accessories and can aid in making any position more comfortable.

 CREATING HOME

Collect your daily wearables with style.

DRESSER TOPS CAN be revealing—or not. For a spare and fresh attitude, a miniature silver tray can elegantly catch your daily wearables, jewelry, or pocket contents. Enhance your simple approach with a single flower in a delicate bottle or vase. If busy and bursting with energy is more your style, use your dressing area to tell your story. Drape necklaces from a mirror frame, hang brilliantly colored scarves in interesting patterns, display a profusion of antique bottles, or show off your collection of fancy beaded handbags.

Rearrange to achieve maximum tranquility.

IF SPACE PERMITS, experiment with new positions for your furniture while keeping the principles of feng shui, the ancient Chinese art of placement, in mind. Practitioners of this ancient art believe that through the placement of furniture, mirrors, crystals, water, rocks, chimes, and plants within a given space, energy blockages can be opened and *chi*, or energy, can be directed in a positive direction. Because your bedroom is the most personal room in your home—where you feel the safest; where you are the most comfortable; where you relax, sleep, and recharge your energies—the placement of objects within your room should inspire the tranquil and peaceful flow of energy. A wind chime hung inside, for example, can help chi circulate more freely about the room. An important tip: make sure that when laying in bed, your feet are not pointing toward the door—your positive chi might walk right out while you are sleeping!

CREATING HOME

*Surround yourself with the necessities
for a perfect slumber.*

YOUR BEDSIDE TABLE should feature items you deem essential
to your most contented state of relaxation. Other than a
bedside lamp and a clock, try to limit your
bedside table items to just a few things—too
much clutter next to your place of rest
can disrupt the harmony of your
quiet haven. A few special items
to consider keeping close at hand:
a small framed picture of a loved
one or a favorite place, a
diminutive jar of rich hand or foot
lotion, a petite vase holding a fresh
rose blossom.

Create a personal reading retreat.

THERE IS NO better place to curl up with a good book or magazine than in your own private space, tucked away from the hectic everyday goings-on within your household. The ideal reading retreat includes a comfy chair, a side table to hold a cup of warm tea, a small lamp for proper illumination, and a small blanket or throw to warm cold feet as needed. If the space within your bedroom won't permit the addition of a chair and table, dedicate a space on your bedside table for your reading gear.

Let soft, twinkling lights lull you to sleep at night.

GROWN-UP night-lights can be relaxing and a welcome change to a totally dark room. Use small white holiday lights in your sanctuary, wrapped around a curtain rod, draped over a plant, or tacked above a window, to create a sky full of stars within your bedroom. A novel idea: put small, glow-in-the-dark reflecting star stickers inside a lampshade. Turn off the lights, then fall asleep to a dreamy celestial glow.

Necessities:
The Home Office

"To business that we love we rise betime, and go to't with delight."
—*William Shakespeare*

WHETHER YOUR OFFICE is a room all its own or is limited to a corner of a table in your living room or kitchen, chances are your work space is becoming a more frequently used portion of your home. Does your work space *look* like the rest of your home? It's easy to skimp on the attention paid to what is essentially a room—or space—of utility. Regardless of how industrial-looking a desk, computer, or filing cabinet may seem, your home office doesn't have to be devoid of style and personality. With a little ingenuity, you can transform your work space to inspire creativity and productivity without sacrificing your decorating panache.

Welcome the organic into your work area.

A MINIATURE HERB garden containing rosemary, thyme, and sage is an ideal organic addition to any work space. The scents, even when fresh, can promote mental agility, concentration, and alertness, and can aid in combating mental fatigue. If you don't have space for an herb garden, find a way to incorporate decorative dried herbs into your design scheme. Create a bouquet garni with a few clips of dried herbs tied with white kitchen string, and place it on your work desk or table. A decorative wreath of dried herbs hung near your desk is another excellent alternative. You'll benefit from the powerful aromatherapy properties of the herbs' essential oils, and your work space will emit a delicious, spicy aroma.

Don't lose the "home" in home office.

HOME OFFICES ARE no longer hidden behind closed doors; in fact, your home work space is increasingly on display. Find clever ways to camouflage office essentials like files, supplies, and reference materials so your office looks like it's a part of your home and your overall design scheme. Style need not be sacrificed in favor of utility or function! An old steamer trunk can hold files, as can a covered rattan basket or an antique picnic basket. A trio of round hatboxes or a grouping of colorful antique tins can hold office supplies and computer cords. A tall stack of weathered leather suitcases can hold reference books and makes for a funky printer stand or side table.

Light your desk with flair.

WHY SETTLE FOR a standard-issue desk lamp when a decorative lamp can illuminate your work space with style. Tag sales, flea markets, church bazaars, and second-hand stores provide great opportunities for unearthing a vintage lamp like a classic brass candlestick, an exotic Oriental floral urn, or an ornate Victorian Gothic. Look beyond any dust, dings, and broken switches— lamps are relatively inexpensive to repair and easy to clean. Add a new hand-stitched linen shade and voilà, you'll have a work light with character.

Turn an everyday item into an unearthed treasure.

Use the right chair.

AS TEMPTING AS it might be to adopt an extra dining room or kitchen chair for home office use, it's not a good idea. Ergonomics are important and if you spend even a minimal amount of time in your office, your body deserves proper support. Your local office supply or office furniture store is bound to have a large selection of desk chairs in varying supports, heights, functions, and price ranges. Unfortunately, sometimes what's comfortable isn't always beautiful. In this instance, function and comfort should take precedence over appearance. A favorite shawl or afghan can give even the most ergonomically functional of chairs your signature style.

Personalize your office accessories.

SOME OFFICE necessities need to be kept readily available;
pens, pencils, computer disks, paper clips, and scratch paper
will probably serve you best if kept right at hand. Create your
own desk accessories for these items by finding new and
interesting uses for objects that fit into your design style. A
blue-tinted antique canning jar might make the perfect holder
for pens, pencils, and scissors if you favor country style; a sleek
stainless cup can serve the same duties if your tastes lean more
to the modern. Experiment with different shapes and sizes and
forge your own signature style.

Refill without running.

YOUR HOME OFFICE probably has all the conveniences of a high-rise office—except a coffee station. Skip all those trips back and forth to the kitchen by setting up your own. Place on a tray: your favorite coffee cup, a thermos brimming with freshly brewed coffee, sugar and powdered creamer, a small basket holding several spoons and napkins, a small vase showcasing a single flower, and a spoon rest. Keep the tray on top of your file cabinet or bookcase and enjoy your java!

Or your favorite tea . . .

Remember your sense of play.

THOUGH YOUR OFFICE is a space intended for serious pursuits, all work and no play can make your work area rather dull. Liven it up by adding a touch of the whimsical. The home office is the perfect place to display the toys you were crazy about as a kid—dolls, teddy bears, matchbox cars, your baseball card collection. Better yet, keep some "modern" toys handy for play today—Koosh balls, chiming Chinese meditation balls, wind chimes—and use them to relieve stress or inspire creative thought when you're burning the midnight oil to meet a deadline. Plus, toys make a great distraction for any visitors—big or small—who may invade your work space.

Tune in.

MUSIC, WHEN PLAYED in the background at a gentle tone, boosts most worker's productivity. Isn't it time to give your office output a jump start? A small clock radio or portable CD player is a welcome addition to any home office. Be sure to select tunes and musical styles that best suit your personal taste and match the tasks at hand.

*Increase home office creativity
and concentration with music!*

Abundance: The Garden

"Happiness is to hold flowers in both hands."
—*Japanese proverb*

GARDEN CAN BE an attitude as well as a space. Real outdoor spaces—like gardens and yards, even decks, patios, balconies, or porches—are an extension of your home and should be treated like outdoor rooms. Make sure your pursuit of comfort and cultivation of your signature style extends beyond the back door.

Accessorize.

LIKE A ROOM within your home, your outdoor space
needs to be accessorized in order to feel complete. Just a
single outdoor accessory—a piece of garden statuary,
perhaps—can tame a wild space and draw it closer to the
confines of home. Birdfeeders, birdhouses, an outdoor
clock or thermometer, beautiful flower pots, or window
boxes—by adding and personalizing these small details,
you can transform your outdoor area into a space
reflective of your home's unique personal style.

Attract the wonders of wildlife.

ENJOY YOUR OWN outdoor wildlife sanctuary by tempting the taste buds of your natural neighbors. Hang squirrel-proof birdfeeders of different sizes to attract hoards of feathered friends. Strategically placed birdbaths and birdhouses will entice feathered friends to stay, sunbathe, and sing. Remember to add a brick or large stone to extend above the surface of the water in your birdbath, so your feathered friends have a place to perch. Tempting suets of corn and sunflower seeds beguile even the shyest chipmunk or squirrel, setting the stage for playful antics. Wildlife is waiting for your invitation.

Nurture yourself with nature.

Celebrate the outdoors with soft sounds.

BELLS AND CHIMES bring sounds of joy to every space, but balconies, decks, and yards offer the greatest potential for sound. When the wind blows, chimes fill your outdoor space with cheery melodies.

Strive for balance.

WHEN YOU MIX stone and sand, along with a water source, among your garden plantings, you create a balance more reflective of nature and hence, a more complete world in which to relax. Larger rocks placed in a bed of sand or gravel add texture reminiscent of a Japanese garden, and can become a spiritual, meditative space.

CREATING HOME

Cultivate a garden of sentiments.

WHETHER YOU PLANT annuals or perennials, tend an Edwardian clipping garden, or simply fill a few window boxes and pots with cheerful blooms, getting to know the symbols, sentiments, and messages of the flowers you choose to plant can enhance your enjoyment and deepen your appreciation for the plants. A kitchen window box of pansies may be a modest, simple display, but pansies, for instance, are also associated with thoughts and thoughtfulness. The hearty pansy implies, *I am thinking of you.* Let your choice of garden blossoms say something about you and your home. Here's a list of the meanings and symbols associated with many popular planting flowers.

74

ABUNDANCE: THE GARDEN

Yellow daffodil: *respect, chivalry*

Red tulip: *declaration of love*

Iris: *I have a message for you*

Daisy: *innocence*

Lily of the valley: *return of happiness*

Azalea: *ephemeral passion; also the Chinese emblem of womanhood*

Red rose: *true love*

White rose: *silence, spiritual; I'm worthy of you*

Yellow rose: *friendship*

Pink rose: *sweetness, trust*

Scarlet geranium: *consolation*

Red chrysanthemum: *remember me; long life and happiness*

White chrysanthemum: *fidelity, truth*

Zinnia: *thoughts of absent friends*

Don't let the out-of-doors limit your seating choices.

COMFORTABLE OUTDOOR seating is a must if you're planning to fully enjoy your home's outdoor space. Benches, lawn chairs, and chaise lounges are standard outdoor fare, but don't let your choices stop there. Your outdoor room can accommodate indoor furniture, too. How about a small daybed or settee on the balcony? An oversized wicker armchair and ottoman, complete with fabric cushions, for the patio? With an eye to the skies, bring a comfy seat from inside, outside. An evening of stargazing on the back porch might be all the nicer when viewed from a stately high-backed Windsor chair from the dining room.

Occasions

"Oh, the fun at arriving at a house and feeling the spark that tells you that you are going to have a good time."
—*Mark Hampton*

ANY TIME FRIENDS, family, and even newcomers are welcomed in to share the bounty of your table, the pleasure of your company, and the comfort of your home, an occasion is in the making. Occasions, be they large or small, monumental or everyday, call for extraspecial details. Whatever the reason, whatever the season, make sure that your occasions are memorable for you and for your guests. Here are a few suggestions for small, special details in every room of your home to help inspire your own traditions for festive occasions.

Guest books are a wonderful way to help your guests feel welcome.

THEY SAY, "WE'RE glad you're here, and we want to remember your visit." Put a guest book or lovely blank book on your table by the door. If the table is a tall one, it will be easier for people to write in as they enter your home. Don't forget the pen! For special occasions, open your book to a fresh page and add your personal note at the top: "Thanks for helping us celebrate Jim's 40th!" or "You're making our 10th Anniversary special!"

Create a special ambiance of comfort by stocking up on extra pillows.

AS GUESTS GATHER and mingle into your living room, expand your seating spaces with floor pillows. Use a rich mix of fabrics, textures, and colors that complement your design scheme and offer soft, luxuriant invitations for comfortable, casual relaxation.

Share your secret ingredients.

AS GUESTS DRIFT into your kitchen, drawn by the smells of a sumptuous meal in the making, offer to share your recipe for the evening fare. A handwritten recipe card including the makings and necessary preparation for one of the dishes on your menu is sure to be treasured by your guests as a reminder of a very special meal.

Let the bounty of your kitchen spread far and wide!

Assign each guest a seat as you gather around the dinner table.

HANDWRITTEN PLACE CARDS, crafted on a heavy card stock and displayed with creative flair, will let every guest know his or her honored seat at your special occasion table. A whimsical place card, written in red ink on bright yellow paper, can be placed on the back of each chair for a casual summer meal. Or try using small fruit, like a lemon, lime, or small apple, to mark each place. Simply cut a very small slice in the fruit and use it to hold firmly the handwritten place marker.

*Simple luxuries in the bath can
mark a special occasion.*

SET OUT A SELECTION of beautiful small hand soaps in an array
of fragrances and colors, some hand-embroidered fingertip
towels, and a small jar or bottle of a rich hand cream. Light a
small aromatherapy votive, too. Guests will emerge from your
bath feeling pampered and refreshed.

*Treat your guests to a tiny
private oasis in the bath.*

Create a special sanctuary for overnight guests.

MAKE SURE TO OUTFIT your guestroom with all of the creature comforts for those special friends and family who are welcomed for an overnight stay. Your guests will appreciate a crisply made bed complete with a generous helping of pillows and an extra blanket to ward off a chill; a stack of bath linens; a small vase of fresh flowers; and an alarm clock. An extra robe and pair of slippers in the closet and a small selection of bath and shower products will be further evidence of your generous hospitality. Don't forget a nightlight or flashlight, to ensure that your guests can find their way safely to the bath (or to the kitchen for a midnight snack) without incident when the lights are low.

84

Make a necessary meeting a home office occasion.

SOMETIMES A MEETING calls for something special. If you work from a home office, this space, too, can be called to service for an occasion to celebrate. Consider tea and cookies with a special client or customer; a morning meeting might include a light breakfast of homemade blueberry muffins to celebrate the completion of a long-term project or the signing of a new contract. Remember, even Dr. John Dolittle (Hugh Lofting's famous animal doctor from Puddleby-on-the-Marsh) served tea every afternoon at his post office and his circus!

C R E A T I N G   H O M E

Abundant light can make your outdoor space festive year-round.

REGARDLESS OF THE season or holiday, your outdoor "room" can always look festive if you keep occasional lighting on hand. Holiday luminarias, those small paper bags weighted with sand and containing small votive candles (electric versions are available, too) look beautiful any time of year. Luminarias can line your patio or deck for a garden party in mid-July or softly illuminate your front walk for a Halloween gathering in late autumn. Small white outdoor lights can be wrapped around a

fence, light post, or porch overhang to add charming twinkles of light with the flip of a switch. Find a favorite festive outdoor light source and use it for every occasion.

"Though all around this mansion high
   Invites the foot to roam,
   And though its halls are fair within—
   Oh, give me back my HOME!"

—"Home"
   Anne Bronte